WALLS
OF CHANGE
THE STORY OF THE WYNWOOD WALLS

For Janet.
She will forever be Tony's
favorite work of art.

WALLS
OF CHANGE
THE STORY OF THE
WYNWOOD WALLS

JESSICA GOLDMAN SREBNICK

TEXT BY HAL RUBENSTEIN

PHOTOGRAPHY BY MARTHA COOPER

ASSOULINE

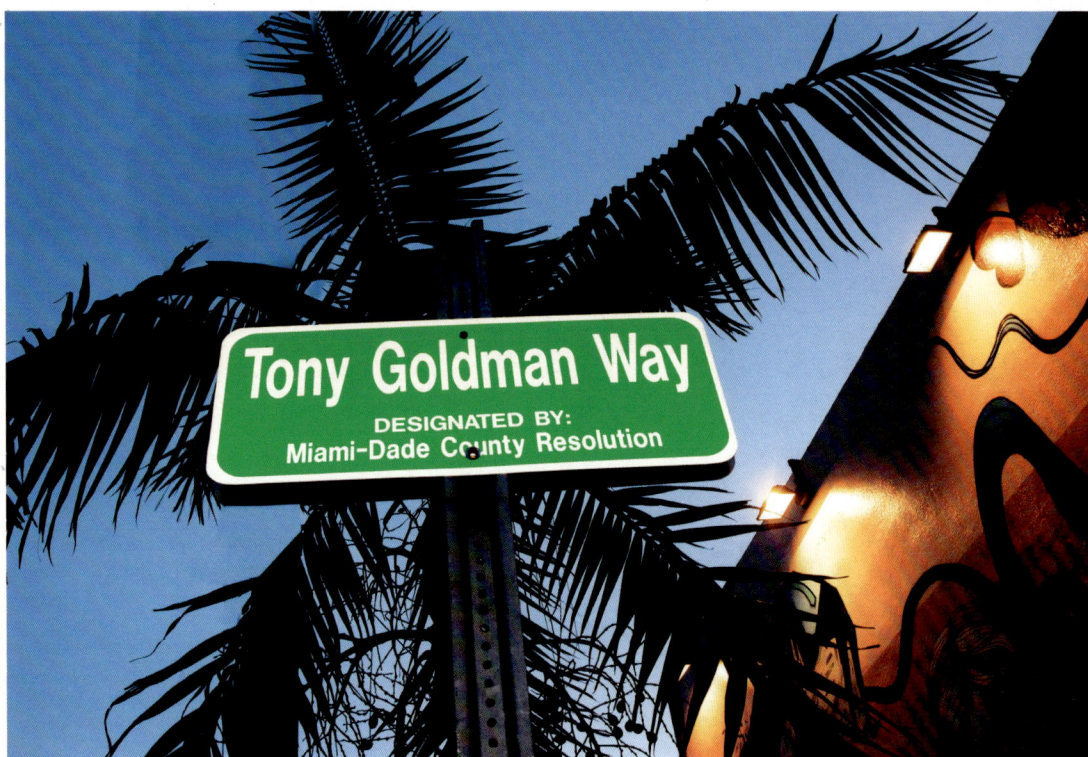

> 66 **THE SECRET INGREDIENT IS INSTINCT—INSTINCT, PASSION AND THE ABILITY TO DO THE UNPREDICTABLE.** 99
>
> TONY GOLDMAN

CONTENTS

FOREWORD
page 8

INTRODUCTION
page 13

2009
page 29

2010
page 51

2011
page 65

2012
page 89

2013
WOMEN ON THE WALLS
page 105

2014
THE ART OF COLLABORATION
page 125

2015
WALLS OF CHANGE
page 145

2016
FEARLESS
page 175

2017
HUMANKIND
page 195

2018
BEYOND WORDS
page 225

ARTIST INDEX
page 252

> **66 WHEN WE LOOK AT A SPACE, WE SEE THE TRUTH IN IT. GOLDMAN PROPERTIES CREATES MAGIC IN PLACES OTHERS OVERLOOK. 99**
>
> TONY GOLDMAN

FOREWORD

By FRANKLIN SIRMANS

Director, Pérez Art Museum Miami

Miami's entrance into the art world began with global attention being directed to public spaces. It was 1983, when Christo wrapped islands in Biscayne Bay in pink fabric, which was organized by our museum's founding director. That was followed by Ed Ruscha's project that encircled the rotunda of the Miami-Dade Public Library with seven paintings that featured a quote from Shakespeare's *Hamlet*. Then there's Claes Oldenburg and Coosje van Bruggen's sliced and peeling orange in Downtown Miami.

We aren't New York, Boston or Chicago. We don't have antiquities and few of our works of art date from before World War II. We're a new big city. We have great collectors but they're not necessarily donating classic works to our museums. Without this historical baggage, it made sense for Miami to look to contemporary art as our foundation.

But it also feels right that Miami should take advantage of its unique geography and environment. Our insistent sun, expansive sky and ever-present sea create a desire to be outside that is inescapable. In cities like New York, Boston and Chicago, they expand museums that often have been built around a core of Greco-Roman architecture. But even their new wings are basically closed-off galleries.

Previous pages: A blank canvas awaits a crew of young street artists.
Following pages: Brilliantly colored tiles laid out for artist Haas & Hahn to compose their wall.

For our new building, architects Herzog & de Meuron created a design that is fluidly inside/outside. Our walls are open to see the sky, and our art is not just hung on the walls. It's readily incorporated into the landscaping.

My background is in contemporary art placed in the public eye, and often created within an urban space. What drew me to contemporary art is that it doesn't exist in and of itself. It reflects and comments on our current culture, and hopefully tells us something about the moment in which we live in this world. In part, that's why it's been fascinating to watch Wynwood's evolution.

It's an incredible thing, the way my friend Jessica Goldman Srebnick has approached Wynwood, and especially The Walls, as an environment rather than a retail enterprise. There is the constant bloom of recognition in this sanctioned space, where artists strive to be seen by more people than ever before, because they have a message. Jessica has been keenly aware and mindful that this generation of artists, whatever their medium, has a profound interest in the way we think about the world. Both of us are happily in agreement that by presenting their work in a thoughtful and curated way, we can bring everyone into a global conversation.

INTRODUCTION

By HAL RUBENSTEIN

I t's no surprise that the essays and quotes in this book are replete with praise for Tony Goldman, justly hailing not only his prophetic vision for The Wynwood Walls, but also referencing his daring yet pragmatic prescience as an urban planner on par with such revered civic sages as Jane Jacobs and Kevin Lynch. Since I was lucky enough to call Tony my friend, it was a joy to chronicle and collate this cascade of heartfelt hosannas and shout-outs of appreciation and gratitude expressed by his colleagues, family and especially, the extended family of street artists proud to be forever associated with The Walls.

However, when talking to a good friend, one's curriculum vitae isn't really a foremost part of your conversations. Rather, what engages you time after happy time is this special person's energy, curiosity, humor, spirit and in Tony's case, his uncanny gift for beguiling you into believing in his dreams. I guess that's why I never regarded Tony as a big-time developer. Instead, I place him alongside Merlin, Houdini, the genie in Aladdin's lamp and Cinderella's fairy godmother, because Tony Goldman was a beneficent magician, a Hogwarts-worthy, "how'd-he-do-that?" sorcerer with the power to conjure new horizons and manifest fresh landscapes not with blueprints, but with a brain wired for wonder.

Tony never sent a saliva swab into 23andMe, but I'll bet my Apple stock that he's descended from Scheherazade, because once those big eyes began sparkling through his glasses, he'd seduce you into seeing things that weren't there yet, stuff you couldn't otherwise imagine. And once he was finished "painting"

At the heart of The Wynwood Walls, the Goldman Properties team creates a gateway for visitors to experience art and culture.
Following pages: Prior to Wynwood's development, glimpses of color and art fill empty streets with inspiration.

Left: Goldman Properties Senior Managing Director Marlo Courtney and Tony Goldman surveying the expanse of stock warehouses in Miami's desolate Wynwood district.

Below: A barren landscape of empty streets and forgotten spaces characterized Wynwood prior to its transformation.

> **"HE GREETED ME WITH THE BUOYANCY OF A MAN WHO HAD SCORED THE DEAL OF A LIFETIME."**
>
> HAL RUBENSTEIN

the picture he wanted you to see—by gesticulating all around you, drawing with his fingers on an imaginary canvas and speaking with the self-satisfied assurance of one who had already paid a visit to this future reality—you were helpless not to become either his disciple, accomplice or cheerleader.

Tony had to stir up a helluva potion to render us bewitched by Wynwood. In Soho, hard and rough as the treeless, cobblestoned area of downtown New York was, he would euphorically rhapsodize over the curves of cast-iron arching above the corniced windows and the artisans crafting beauty behind them until you acquiesced that his home base would become the city's epicenter of sensuality. To Tony, South Beach's modernist Deco and Bauhaus structures were an undeniably irresistible backdrop for seasons beckoning with the promise of sun-kissed romance.

But Wynwood was simply flat and ugly, architecturally and socially inert. Ten years ago, when I first drove there to meet him, I was taunted at a stoplight by a man whose kingdom was a street corner claiming only a fool would cruise these streets with the top down on his convertible. Yet, when I encountered Tony, standing in an empty lot on NW 2nd Avenue near NW 26th Street, he greeted me with the buoyancy of a man who had scored the deal of a lifetime on the choicest waterfront estate in East Hampton. "Boychik, look at this!" Look at what? There was nothing there. And then, Tony started "painting."

That the ever-evolving public art Brigadoon that is The Wynwood Walls opened in 2009 looking almost exactly as Tony conceived it is remarkable enough. That it is acknowledged by street artists around the world as their polestar and that an invitation to participate in The Walls' annual exhibition is communally accepted as their apex of achievement is something that would have tickled and maybe even surprised Tony. But considering the man's unabated desire to embrace those he loved, what would have made him even more deliriously

Following pages: Members of The Wynwood Walls team laying the groundwork for The Wynwood Walls.

proud is the foresight, ambition, and guts that his daughter Jessica Goldman Srebnick, his family, and his team (many of whom you will hear from in these pages) have employed to make this a must-see destination for nearly three million tourists a year.

However, none of these achievements are as singularly astounding as the iconoclastic road map that Tony Goldman devised to make Wynwood one of the most exciting and perhaps influential neighborhoods in the country. The usual process of creating a viable urban plan is well-tested and methodical. Housing first, followed by commerce, then amenities, and finally culture.

For Wynwood, Tony did just the opposite. He went back to front. So exhilarated and invested was he in the potential of this commanding new art form, brimming with stunning, innovative imagery, driven by talented, committed artists eager to convey messages that were vital and personal, yet relatable and universal, that against all logic he proclaimed his love for street art would be the foundation for Wynwood's success.

We have all read enough to know that sorcerers are powerful. But the rare sorcerer whose secret ingredient is love is as join-in-or-get-out-of-his-way unstoppable as he is irresistible. Tony's enthusiasm for what he loved was titanic, daunting and electrifying. That's why the output from Wynwood's decade of presentations supersedes any kaleidoscope you've ever peered through. The included recollections and memories of dozens of our featured artists and passionate collaborators are informative and unapologetically emotional, and boast so many personal riffs as to rival the improvisational rhythms of jazz great Charlie Parker. We're hoping this book works a little of The Wynwood Walls magic on you. Tony would have liked that.

A composition of place, people, art and energy, Tony Goldman's vision shaped Wynwood into an internationally recognized destination for culture and community.

> **❝ I THINK IN A FORMER LIFE I WAS AN EXPLORER. I LIKE BEING FIRST OUT ON THE PLAINS. ❞**
>
> TONY GOLDMAN

JESSICA GOLDMAN SREBNICK

CEO, Goldman Properties
Founder, Goldman Global Arts
Curator, Wynwood Walls

My entire life, I was a student of one of the greatest visionaries and urban placemakers this country has ever known: my father, Tony Goldman. He was the consummate entrepreneur and risk-taker, someone who was not afraid to put his money and reputation on the line every day, daring to be bold, to be different, to be a contrarian, to push forward when the naysayers told him he was crazy ... and a lot of people told him that he was crazy. You see, people don't always understand big, optimistic thinkers.

In October of 2009, Dad's mind-set was different from when he was developing Soho, South Beach or Center City in Philadelphia. He had survived a double lung transplant the year prior. Every breath was a gift appreciated like never before. His intensity and his drive were all focused in one direction. He had just enough oxygen to breathe life into his ultimate masterpiece; Wynwood would be his final legacy.

To me, the story of Wynwood is not just about discovering a new neighborhood and taking financial risks. It's not about cap rates and NOIs and return on investment. It's about pursuing passion, thinking creatively, differentiating ourselves, elevating others, doing the unexpected and leading by example. It's about improving the quality of life for people on the street.

It's about capturing the image of a desolate neighborhood in a mind's eye and seeing the potential of what could be. It's about

taking the torn fabric of a neighborhood and lovingly mending it. It's about finding the courage to open a restaurant called Joey's when there was no proven market. It's about providing financial assistance to a local baker with a fabulous product to help him succeed because his success is integral to ours. It's about dedicating two acres of prime real estate, in the epicenter of the neighborhood, and converting them into a public space—an international outdoor museum—to elevate a form of art that had never received public recognition. It's about changing the way people experience art and appreciating the historically maligned street artists whose works grace our walls. It's about celebrating creativity and encouraging kindness and collaboration. It's about igniting the conversation in the art world and beyond through our thought-provoking themes. It's about being committed to a project that has taken on a life of its own. The Wynwood Walls has changed the trajectory of careers and catapulted this genre of art into another stratosphere. This project has inspired both the youngest and oldest and every age in between to see the world differently. The Wynwood Walls is a celebration of art that not only informs, but uplifts the human spirit.

Street artists are a particularly courageous bunch. In the dark of the night, often illegally, they make their mark with a can of spray paint. Historically, graffiti has been viewed as a symbol of destruction and vandalism. People like my father and Jeffrey

Deitch saw graffiti through a different lens; they recognized that the artists creating this work were looking for an outlet. They had something to say, something to share. They had big ideas and increasingly superior execution, and we had big canvases. Today, I scan the world, eyes wide open, looking for artistic talent, so that we can add to our growing family of artists and projects. From Lithuania to Brazil, Japan to Mexico, Norway to Germany, there is meaningful, experimental and beautiful work happening, and we have brought that perspective to Wynwood.

My dad always said that no matter how hard you strive to create or build something, once you put it out there, it takes on a life of its own. The Walls are bigger and more popular than anyone in my family could have ever dreamed. What started as a gravel parking lot now sees more than three million visitors a year entering its gates. What differentiates this space is that the energy of the artists lingers well after the paint has dried. My father's energy is there. My energy is there. There are many people who have contributed to the magic of The Walls, and in doing so have made a positive contribution to the world. Together, we have created a global destination that celebrates creativity. That is a legacy to be deeply proud of.

To me, the greatest compliments I receive are when I hear people proclaim that there is nowhere in the world quite like Wynwood,

Soho, Philadelphia or Miami Beach. I take such pride when I see the range of age and nationality walking the streets of these once decayed and abandoned neighborhoods. Places once void of energy are now bustling with creativity, people and purpose.

At the end of my father's sixty-eight years on Earth, I gained a deep sense of gratitude for the gift of life, the extraordinary liberties we enjoy in this country and the meaning of commitment. The world was blessed that "Tony was here." We hope that those who spend time at The Walls will come away more hopeful about the future, more willing to infuse creativity into the world, and with the desire to take on the personal responsibility of making the world a more beautiful, inclusive and interesting place, in their very own way.

JOEY GOLDMAN

Partner, Goldman Properties
Co-founder of Wynwood and Wynwood Walls

When I moved my family down to Miami in 2001, South Beach was white-hot. So, Dad sent me out on a search for a new neighborhood. We first looked near the Bass museum and further north on the beach, but we're developers, not high-rise apartment builders, which is what those areas were attracting. One day in 2005, I found myself in Wynwood. It was a neighborhood in ruins: empty warehouses, no commercial business, no parking, no street life.

There was the start of an art movement there, but the infrastructure to create a neighborhood didn't exist. I started to do the groundwork there, so we could, as Dad called it, "play Monopoly." The area was zoned only for

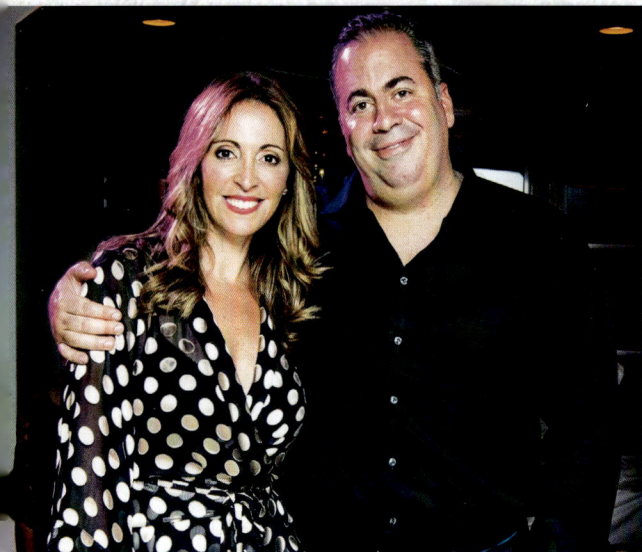

industrial use. Still, we planted a stake. I opened the first restaurant in Wynwood, Joey's. Almost immediately, a bullet hit the building. This wasn't going to be easy.

We bought the area for The Walls in 2007. Dad came up with the idea of painting all the buildings we'd bought around it. We lobbied for rezoning, liquor licenses and the rights to come up with a café district. We were determined. The way Dad taught us to work was it was never a question of "if," just "when."

When we opened, people were surprised we didn't charge to get into The Walls, but that's not us. Dad loved street art, he loved all forms of creativity, and he got the biggest kick out of building a neighborhood where there wasn't one. But Dad loved people more than anything. That's why it's perfect that Shepard Fairey's mural of him has his arms wide open and welcoming. He relished any chance to have people experience something new.

The Walls became the center of our new neighborhood because they continue to offer the ultimate opportunity for creative people to express and be themselves. The result of this rare collaboration is that we're presenting the best example of the human spirit at the top of its game.

JANET GOLDMAN

Chairman and Principal, Goldman Properties

Tony believed in art of and for the people. Whenever he had a vision, he would take a plunge into a big idea. He thrived on the discovery and the commitment, and the rush of love at first sight. But Tony didn't just dream. I remember that he wrote in his journal that "if vision isn't actualized and executed as intended, it's merely daydreaming." For the big ideas to be realized, you had to back it up with press, navigate the politics, form a coalition of power players and community, and drive the economics.

Wynwood was a unique challenge, probably Tony's biggest. Because unlike South Beach or Soho, there was no beach, no city center, no historic fabric, not even any people. But the buildings were human scale, there were no tall structures (I always thought Tony was a little bit claustrophobic), the streets were wide and the light was magnificent.

Tony didn't like being called a visionary because he thought it sounded arrogant and presumptuous, but that's exactly what he was. He may have been a businessman, but he combined it with being a mentor and a communicator. He didn't start with a plan. Instead, he waited for an emotional inspiration. Once the passion hit him, he'd say to himself, "Do I have the balls to take the risk?" If the answer was an emphatic "Yes!" that would drive him to plan.

In the winter of 2008, Tony and Jeffrey Deitch agreed to collaborate on The Wynwood Walls. Jeffrey had turned him on to what he believed was art's next wave: art performed out of doors that was raw, renegade and spontaneous. The more Tony was exposed to it, the more exuberant he became.

When Joey first took us to Wynwood, some street art was already there, though most of it was random. But Tony was always a quick study. He started buying street art books, checking out what contemporaries were doing, and realized he could bring this to a higher level than anyone else had. He saw a happening, but in a safe space where all these great artists could do their own thing. He imagined the electricity generated by artists stimulating each other while creating.

Though he's labeled a developer, Tony was actually in the hospitality business. It was an extension of his personality to satisfy and entertain. To him, art wasn't an extravagance. It was married into every project he did, because art brings color, light and happiness. Tony wasn't greedy. He made room for others to participate in his vision. And now, our daughter has raised the aesthetic bar, yet maintains this pedestrian-friendly place for exploring, dining and discovery. Everyone around us has benefited because of what our family has done and will proudly continue to do in order to create a destination where people are happy to be. "Feed the neighborhood, and the neighborhood will feed you," Tony always said. Wynwood is exactly as Tony imagined it would be. And that's why I loved him.

SCOTT SREBNICK

Special Advisor, Goldman Properties

In 1966, like so many other Cubans who came to Miami, my family settled in Wynwood, where my parents opened a big zipper factory. Eventually, we became distributors for YKK, the zipper giant. My mom could tell you all the names of the clothing manufacturers that once occupied the buildings the Goldmans later bought because they were our clients. One by one they left to Asia, Central America and the Caribbean, in search of cheap labor.

When Tony started looking around Wynwood to buy up property in 2005, he asked my mom to invest. She said, "You are crazy. Why don't you buy our property? I see no future here." How did we not buy into Tony's vision? It was so hard for us to see it. But, man, what he could see!

When the recession hit in 2008, even more companies closed up shop. Tony was paying property tax on empty buildings. Tony's solution to this problem was crazy and unique, but then he relished the obstacle of people telling him he couldn't do something.

Unlike other developers, Tony didn't initially consider how things would work financially. Imagine telling a potential investor you're going to create a neighborhood by letting artists paint all over the walls of empty buildings because that would spark interest. But Tony believed that if you developed something unique, creative people would want to be there. Tony believed in himself; he had an unwavering confidence in his own vision.

He brought in the artists. He gave the Museum of Contemporary Art a four-year lease for $1 a year. He gave space to Panther Coffee and Zak the Baker and loaned money to start-ups with very little credit because he knew by differentiating the neighborhood he'd attract more businesses.

At the time, Tony was going through health issues. He realized his time was limited; not exactly the best moment for major risk-taking. Tony didn't care. In fact, his most creative period was the year after he had two new lungs in his body. Happiness was bursting out of him. "This is my signature project. This is what they will remember me for."

When Jessica took over after Tony's passing in 2012, she decided that every year we'd create a theme to focus the artists' power. We were also going to make these artists feel appreciated and honored, inviting them into our home and featuring them at events. Jessica helped many get noticed, promoted them on social media and celebrated their enormous talent, and they, of course, allowed The Walls to take off.

Jessica is only beginning to realize the influence she wields, because what her family has created is now known worldwide. It's funny. She will see someone on Instagram in Lithuania, call him, and say, "Hi, I'm the curator of The Wynwood Walls," and she'll sense the artist's excitement on the other end. When an artist gets a call from Jessica, it's like Willy Wonka giving out a Golden Ticket.

MARLO COURTNEY

Senior Managing Director, Goldman Properties

In 1977, Tony took me to see what he predicted would soon be the hottest supper club in New York City. All I saw was an abandoned transfer station. A year later, Greene Street Cafe was the hit Tony had predicted. My friend had a gift. I went to work for him if only to see what other magic he could do.

In the mid-eighties, Tony discovered Miami Beach, saw an unrecognized American Riviera, and started buying property on and around Ocean Drive. South Beach transformed fast. By the early nineties, the cool people had found it, and they were coming often. The Art Deco hotels became the backdrop for models and photographers shooting for magazines and catalogues. During his six years as chairman of the Greater Miami Convention & Visitors Bureau, Tony worked to promote Miami as an international tourist destination. He was also an enthusiastic promoter of Art Basel Miami Beach, which launched in 2002.

In 2005, it was time to give his son, Joey, a new challenge. He told him to seek out our company's next zone. Joey came back with Wynwood. It was totally desolate. With Joey's scouting as the catalyst, we began buying in

Wynwood. The area was a bit of an open book for us because it was our first time getting involved in a non-historic district. Wynwood had no notable architecture or cultural legacy. The path of least resistance for most builders taking on a neighborhood of warehouse buildings would be gentrification. As usual, Tony went the other way.

Combining Tony's passion with Jeffrey Deitch's connections, the two new friends conspired to make Wynwood a world-class location for international street artists.

In addition to believing in his gut, Tony believed in "the grid." For a neighborhood to succeed, he had to be able to locate a potential "Main Street," and he determined Wynwood's spine would be NW 2nd Avenue, and its heart would be on 26th Street in a gravel parking lot. Tony immediately envisioned a park. An art park.

He then sought out the street artists whom he and Jeffrey loved. Scharf, Shepard, Futura, Stelios Faitakis, Retna, Ara Peterson, Nunca. When they asked Tony what they were expected to do, Tony replied, "Give me your best," and they did.

Despite their freedom, artists had to adjust to Tony's idea of public art as an interactive experience. Suddenly, they were experiencing contact with the public during the creative process. It was a big risk to set them up like this. But the artists flipped when they discovered they had fans—truly excited ones. The combination of engagement and nearly unlimited support was electrifying. The Wynwood Walls was successful from the moment it started.

The neighborhood is alive and growing because of a man who believed each of us has the ability to make a difference in the world.

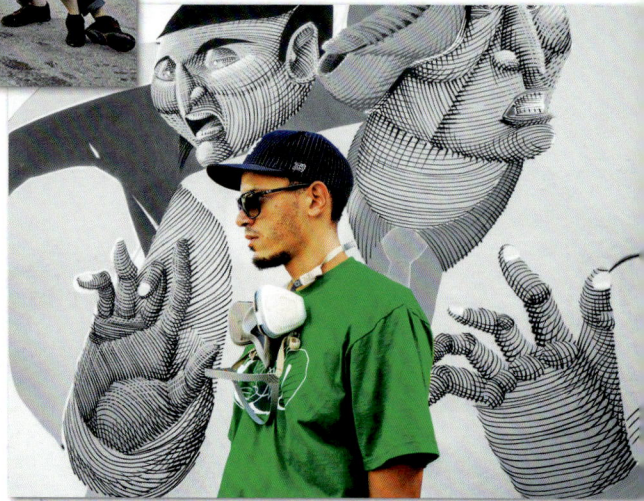

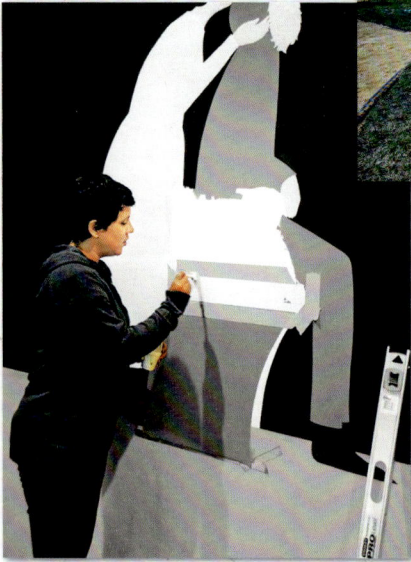

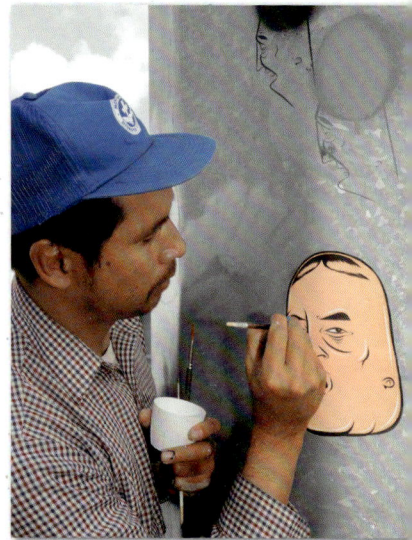

ARA PETERSON
BARRY MCGEE
CLARE ROJAS
FUTURA 2000
JIM DRAIN
KENNY SCHARF
LADY AIKO
NUNCA
OSGEMEOS
SHEPARD FAIREY
STELIOS FAITAKIS
SWOON

2009

JEFFREY DEITCH

Art dealer and curator, former director of the Museum of Contemporary Art, Los Angeles
Curator of the first Wynwood Walls

Tony was the most important personality in Soho. He loved the neighborhood and was vitally engaged with its growth. He began visiting my gallery, soon becoming a regular. But his visits weren't just about buying art. Tony came to talk and to learn.

Tony was particularly interested in the platform I was giving street artists. It was amazingly serendipitous that I represented the Keith Haring estate for thirteen years. Haring had painted this landmark mural in 1982 on a concrete wall on the corner of Houston and the Bowery (he succumbed to AIDS in 1990). But the wall had deteriorated over time, and was finally painted over. While discussing Haring, I asked Tony if he knew who owned that eccentric corner block of concrete.

"I own it!" he replied, and immediately decided we should use it as a curated showcase for street artists. But he wanted to launch the wall by doing something special to mark the fiftieth anniversary of Keith's birth. Thanks to new technology, we recreated Haring's original mural almost twenty-five years later. It was a triumph. Hundreds of people watched it being painted. Hundreds more began coming every day, with most taking photos. (Instagram was still two years away.)

It was also significant because Tony and I realized we could do something important together. He already had a plan. "Come to Miami," he insisted. "You have to see what I'm doing in Wynwood." I went and looked around as he painted vivid, verbal pictures on every empty block. I agreed to curate his concept for the first Wynwood Walls—The outdoor museum of street art.

We dove in. We brought in established artists and mixed them with the next generation. Between Tony's optimistic vision and my prior relationships with these artists, we were able to initiate a dialogue that went beyond inviting them just to do something. We wanted them to do something amazing.

When the artists were finished, people were stunned. Frankly, so were we. It's incredibly rewarding when something you believe in goes beyond your expectations. For the first couple of years, Wynwood Walls was by far the best thing at Art Basel. No one had ever done an outdoor museum at this level, one that boasted artistic rigor but was totally accessible in a location so disarming and open. Even the restaurant Tony opened in the courtyard felt authentic.

More than sixty unofficial versions of Wynwood Walls have sprouted up around the world. I don't think there is anything else I have done that has sparked so many imitators. In addition, the area now boasts ten times the amount of street art. Street artists come from all over the world, with or without permission, because they know their work will be noticed. And their art becomes an economic multiplier.

Tony had the foresight. He understood the architecture of the space, how to lift it up and give the art he wanted featured here dignity and authority. The gates, grassy paths, night lighting, spacious patio—by elevating the landscape, he gave artists and art lovers a platform that had never existed before. When we opened, I remember Tony beaming as the first crowds started pouring in. "Here comes the neighborhood!"

He just knew.

Tony Goldman (left) and Jeffrey Deitch celebrating the first exhibitions at the Wynwood Walls, 2009.

"I REMEMBER JEFFREY DEITCH AND **TONY GOLDMAN** TAKING ME THROUGH **THE WALLS** IN 2009. WE ONLY SAW **EMPTY STORES,** CAR REPAIR SHOPS AND A COFFEE BAR. BUT WE WERE SO EXCITED AND READY TO MAKE SOMETHING NEW, **SOMETHING WOW.**"

LADY AIKO, *Japan*

> ❝ **THROUGH PAINT, ENERGY, AND CREATIVITY, YOU'RE SENDING OUT ELECTRICITY AND IMAGERY THAT ELEVATES.** ❞
>
> TONY GOLDMAN

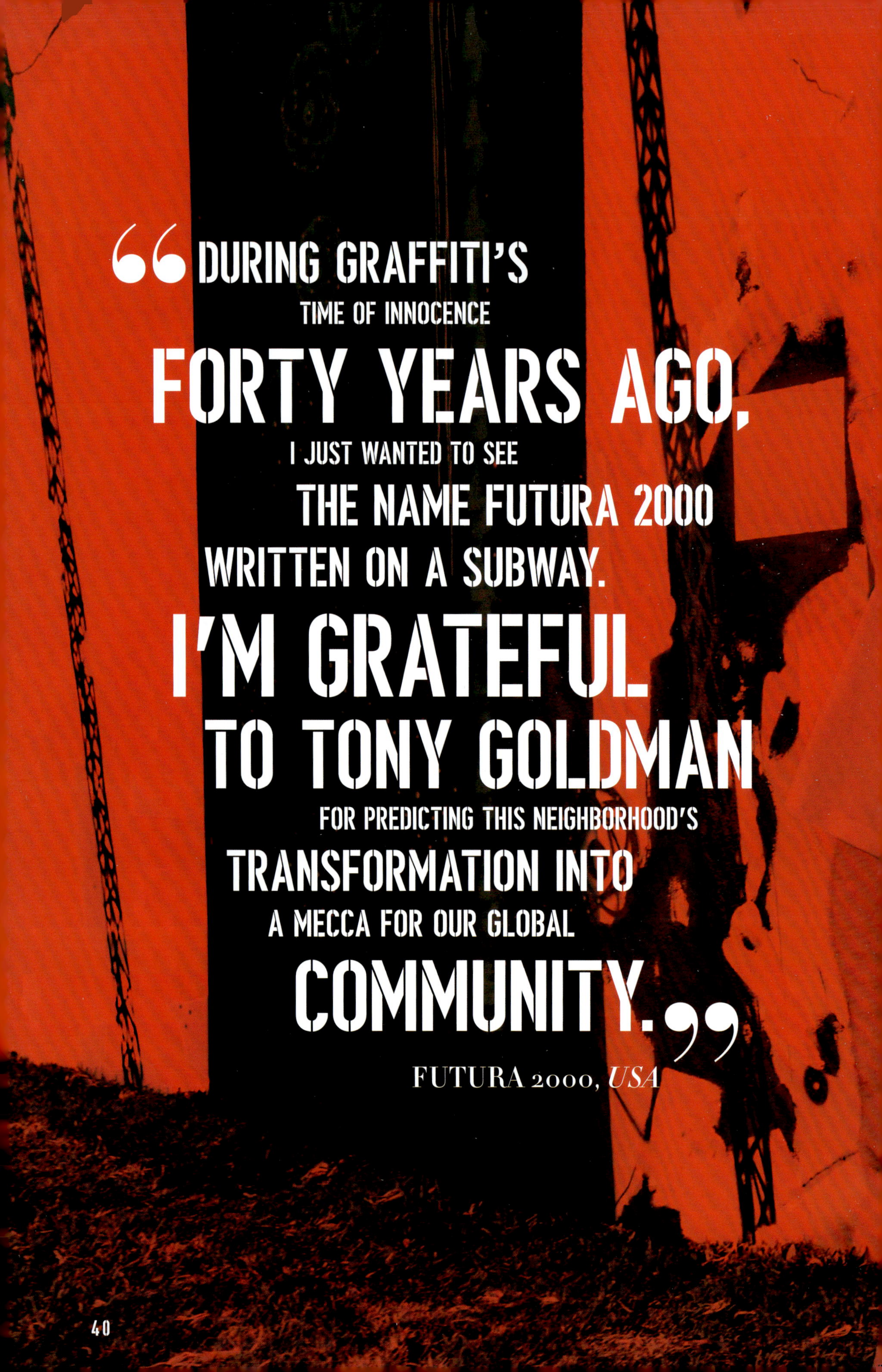

"DURING GRAFFITI'S
TIME OF INNOCENCE
FORTY YEARS AGO,
I JUST WANTED TO SEE
THE NAME FUTURA 2000
WRITTEN ON A SUBWAY.
I'M GRATEFUL
TO TONY GOLDMAN
FOR PREDICTING THIS NEIGHBORHOOD'S
TRANSFORMATION INTO
A MECCA FOR OUR GLOBAL
COMMUNITY."

FUTURA 2000, *USA*

" IT WAS THE FIRST TIME
I EXHIBITED IN THE U.S.
MORE THAN ANYTHING,
I REMEMBER
I WAS TREATED IN A WAY THAT
RAISED MY LEVEL
OF EXPECTATION
FOR A LARGE-SCALE WORK.
IT WAS A
WONDERFUL OPPORTUNITY
TO WORK AND EXHIBIT
WITH ARTISTS I
ADMIRED
AND WHO WERE INFLUENTIAL
IN THE CONTINUATION OF
MY STUDY. "

STELIOS FAITAKIS, *Greece*

KENNY SCHARF

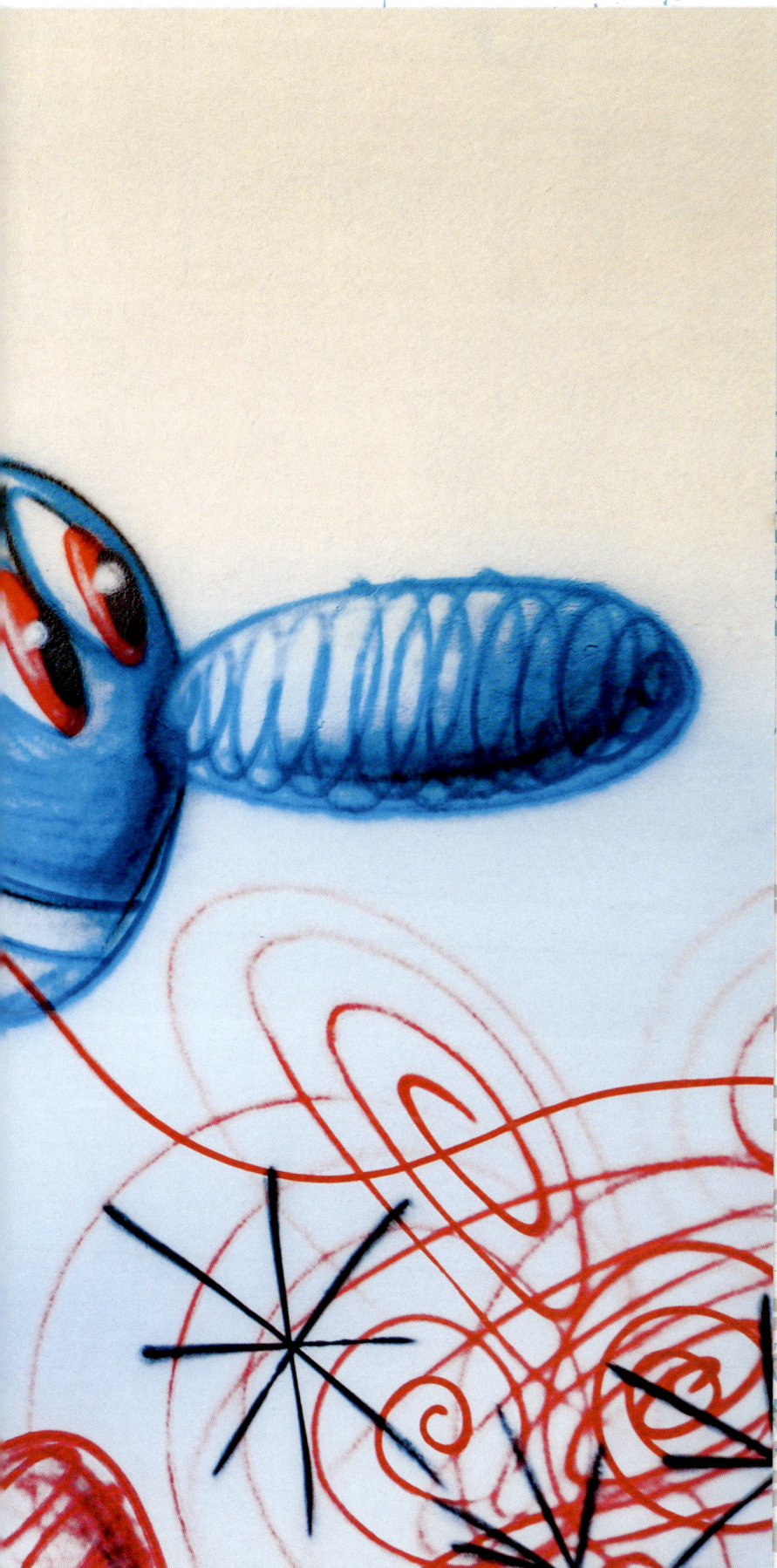

SHEPARD FAIREY

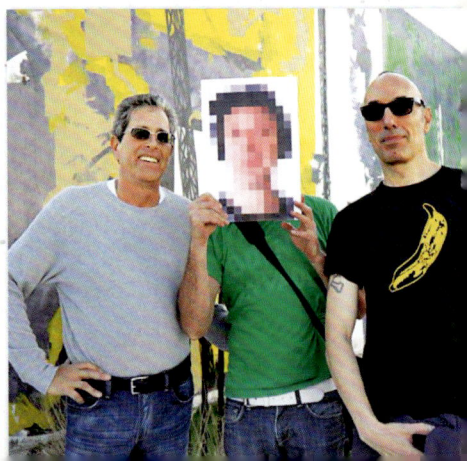

AVAF
BARRY MCGEE
BEN JONES
COCO144
DEARRAINDROP
INVADER
JEFF SOTO
LOGAN HICKS
PHASE 2
RON ENGLISH
RYAN MCGINNESS

2010

The first time I went to Wynwood was in 2010 with Primary Flight, which was kind of a ragtag bunch of artists back then. Between us, we had about eight walls and maybe eight cans of spray paint to work with in this sketchy neighborhood. Looking for something I could do on my own, I found a guy with a mini truck and asked him, "Hey man, can I paint your truck?" He was cool with that, so I painted my Rabbit on the back doors. But that night, someone stole them. And then I found out it wasn't even the guy's truck!

The next year, I went back to Wynwood, commissioned to paint on a building. It wasn't exactly a plum gig. I was given a bucket of black and a bucket of white paint and a ladder with three rungs. I went by The Walls to check them out, and there were lifts and hundreds of gallons of primo paint, and I thought, "Fuck, I want to be over here with Futura and Kenny Scharf. How do I get with this crew?" Later that year, the New York gallery representing me had a group show, so I did this **huge installation** with the Camo Deer and Temper Tot and demanded the gallery owner get Tony to show up.

Tony showed, bought all the Camo Deer, told me he was taking them down to Miami with him, and asked me to paint them and whatever else I wanted on one of the walls.

I got what I wanted! I painted the Temper Tot, and then improvised around him, tracing patterns of a tree, painting a rock and then projecting the Camo Deer on the rock. The Goldmans kept the mural for nine years, with me constantly repainting it, until it got too faded. Tony even gave me his special wall on Houston Street in New York City. **To paint that wall was like getting an Oscar.**

RON ENGLISH

Artist, USA

When Tony passed, I realized that very few people change the world, but he changed our world. He took an area where, at one time, if you parked outside what the police called the "safe zone," your windows got smashed, and developed it counter-intuitively, with his initial focus on installing stuff that wasn't going to generate any money because it was created by unrecognized outsiders in the art world. Tony became our champion, infused us with his spirit and turned all us outsiders into winners.

What's just as cool is that his daughter, Jessica, could have walked away, or kept The Walls as it was, or dropped the ball. Instead, she just keeps increasing the profile, expanding the neighborhood. Just look at what she did with the new parking garage. She commissioned a building that's a giant sculpture, a functioning work of art. It's so wild. **Tony would be insanely proud of her.**

People talk about a cultural divide when it comes to art. Well, yeah, if you spend your life solely in museums. Wynwood creates art for the people. Busloads of them show up these days. That collaboration with both other artists and the public gets your creative juices flowing. In fact, I designed a piece using fluorescence and shadow so that the viewer becomes part of the art, like a reflective pool. Within The Walls, they're up for letting you try anything. It's like Tony threw a stone into this pond, and the rings just keep rippling around it.

A tiny visitor poses in front of Ron English's 2009 mural.

RON ENGLISH

RYAN MCGINNESS

"ANY SIMPLE FORM CAN BE A CANVAS FOR CREATIVITY ... THE MORE UNEXPECTED THE BETTER."

JESSICA GOLDMAN SREBNICK

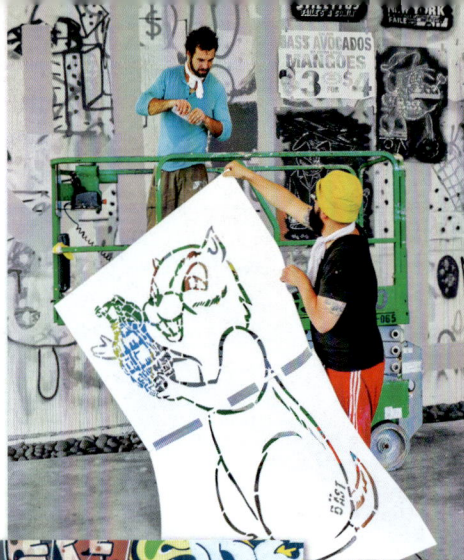

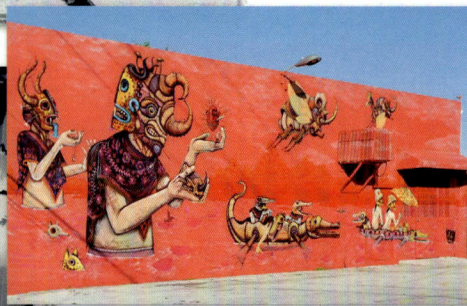

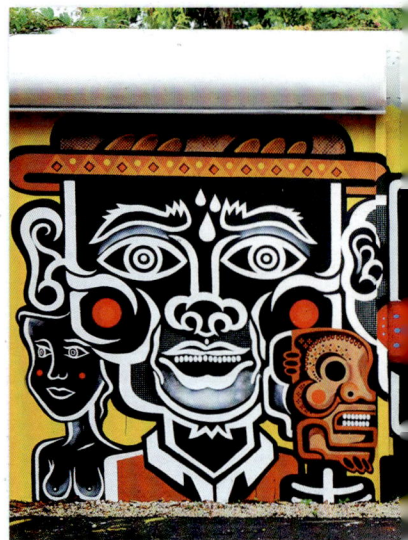

AVAF

B.

BÄST

BRANDON OPALKA

COCO144

DATE FARMERS

DAZE

FAILE

GAIA

HOWNOSM

INTERESNI KAZKI

IRAK

JOE GRILLO

KENNY SCHARF

LIQEN

LOGAN HICKS

NEUZZ

NUNCA

RETNA

ROA

SANER

SEGO

SHEPARD FAIREY

VHILS

2011

PETER TUNNEY

Artist , Co-founder of Goldman Global Arts and Goldman Global Arts Gallery

Other Wynwood-like places have sprung up around the world, and that's good, but the reason why they really can't replicate this is because they don't have Tony's spirit living inside them the way we all do. The man was the embodiment of the power of one. No group can do the same. I hear it constantly, "Peter, we painted thirty murals in our town. Nothing happened. In fact, some of the people in the neighborhood are complaining. What did we do wrong?"

I don't want to laugh because that would be mean. But it was **never simply about the murals.** It was about the intent. There was ambition in what Tony was doing, as well as drive and commerce. But there was also a **purity in its creation** that still infuses Wynwood.

Tony saw this collection of art and artists as a way to create a vibrant and vital neighborhood, one that used art as a way to build a community that believed in activism, collaboration and positive change. You only have to witness what happens every year when the artists come together to see how brilliantly this works.

Want to know something incredible? No one has ever taken so much as a Sharpie to any of these walls, scrawled their initials, or defaced one in any way. Over three hundred thousand visitors come through here during Art Basel with zero incidents of drunkenness or stupidity. You can't say that about the Louvre, or any major cathedral.

What's more, we don't have guards or control by the police. This place is protected by non-stop mutual respect and **never-ending waves of kindness.**

Something else unites the artists who come here. It's inherent in them. It's what Tony saw, and now what Jessica seeks. Their motivation as contemporary artists reflects their concerns about the environment, and about how we treat each other. They don't just depict life as it is. They comment on how it should be.

The fact that guys like Ron English, Futura, Shepard Fairey and so many others who were launched here can make a hell of a living doing this is goddamn incredible. Tony's energy was nuclear. And what we continue to do here is plant and nurture these seeds of humanity and ecological concern that are spreading through like-minded communities throughout the world. Enter The Walls and you'll feel the power of ninety-nine hugs exchanged between ninety-nine people.

It's astounding to me that Tony walked into this parking lot and, being the fearless motherfucker that he was, said with no hesitation, "This is what we're gonna do here. I need to feel a beating heart. I need some time in the sunshine every day, surrounded by good energy." **It's an incredible story.** Now, Jessica is off and running with it, and you can see the fire in her eyes. It just keeps getting better. That's why I don't think I've missed a day of work here in ten years. **This place is a straight-up miracle.**

Goldman Global Arts Co-founder Peter Tunney in front of the GGA Gallery.
Facade installed by Vhils during 2018 Beyond Words art week program.

"WYNWOOD WALLS IS A SAFE HAVEN WHERE MURALS CAN BE CREATED AND EXHIBITED IN A CONTEXT THAT JUST MAKES SENSE. THERE IS A LEVEL OF IMMEDIACY YOU DON'T FIND IN THE STUDIO."

DAZE, *USA*

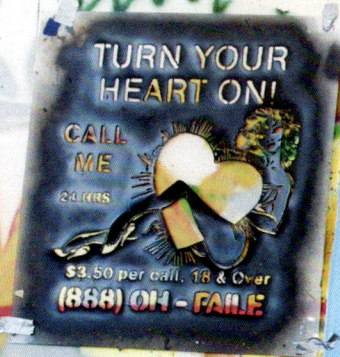

66 MY. BEST. RESPONSE IS. THE. ONE. I THAT TAKES TO MANY. SMILES A FEW TEARS. A MAN. WHOM BREAD MANY. EYE HAVE VISIONS OF. MR. GOLDMAN. A. INNOVATION ON TO HIMSELF. NO OTHER PERSON. HAVE I MET WHOM COULD SEE A MARKET. AND. CARE LESS. CARELESS. HE WAS NOT. MR. GOLDMAN CREATOR OF. SOHO. WYN WOOD. MIAMI BEACH. I REMEMBER TONY BOUGHT MY FIRST MOST EXPENSIVE PIECE. HE ALLOWED ME TO SET A FEW BENCHMARKS. **99**

RETNA, *USA*

"BEING ASKED TO PARTICIPATE IN 2011 WAS A **MILESTONE** FOR US. EVEN IN PRE-INSTAGRAM TIMES, THE EXPOSURE WAS AMAZING, THE PEOPLE WE MET WERE SO COOL, AND THE ARTISTS FREELY SHARED THEIR EXPERIENCES. WYNWOOD WALLS REMAINS THE NO. 1 MURAL PROJECT IN THE WORLD."

INTERESNI KAZKI, *Ukraine*

INTERESNI KAZKI

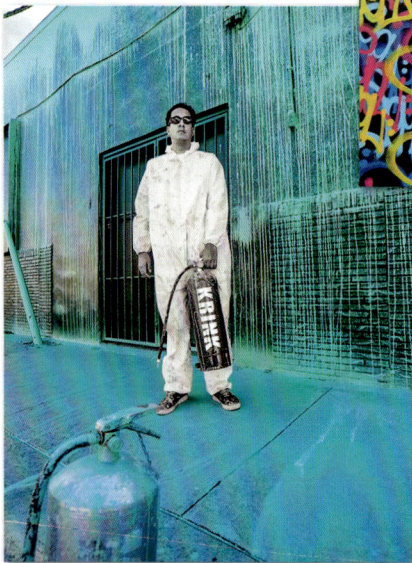

BRANDON OPALKA
DALEAST
DAZE
FAITH47
HOWNOSM
NEMEL
KENNY SCHARF
KRINK
MOMO
POSE
SANTIAGO RUBINO
SHEPARD FAIREY

2012

SHEPARD FAIREY

Artist, USA

When Jeffrey Deitch introduced me to Tony, I didn't know his history. I was in the midst of my evolution as a renegade outsider. "Fuck the banks." "Fuck the police." "Fuck the corporation." I was surprised to find this big developer who was passionate about art in public spaces and determined to find ways of using culture to create a neighborhood.

While talking to him, I began to realize the power of an insider who knows how to use his clout and influence to infiltrate the system and make cool stuff happen. The remarkable thing was that he saw culture and business as collaborators, not in opposition. Suddenly, this renegade saw partnership with Tony as a logical growth.

Public art is really a Trojan horse. Messages that are all purely agitational these days come through like white noise. But what if you can figure out how to deliver the medicine with some sugar? It's quite the incentive to discover how subversive you can be when you are working in a beautiful setting and you can get something really good to eat.

The whole complex of Wynwood is just really well-done. I know I'm biased at this point because most of the artists I've met there have become my friends, plus Tony invited me to paint the interior of Wynwood Kitchen & Bar, but he managed to transmit to us what was possible if street art was handsomely presented.

Andy Warhol, Robert Indiana and Robert Rauschenberg had already proved it to be true, but Wynwood Walls was this sprawling real estate manifesto that proclaimed you absolutely can mix design and art, commerce and communication, and anytime there's an opportunity to mow down the doubters, I'm excited to be counted in.

Though she was involved from the beginning, Jessica was thrown in headfirst right after Tony died, and there was no way she could have known how complex the physical and psychological landmines she'd encounter in navigating all these artists toward a common goal would be. But she is not faint of heart and just keeps moving forward. She didn't have Tony's deep background in the art world, but maybe because she is a big fan with no preconceived notions, she was able to mix things up in several ways that rattled what was becoming orthodoxy in public art.

The speed with which Wynwood achieved critical mass could not have been imagined—this former neighborhood of crackheads and tumbleweeds—but Tony's vision was so clear, and everyone involved with the Goldmans was so in sync, that no effort ever felt wasted. Though it went on for years, the debate about graffiti's legitimacy was invalidated the moment you walked through the Wynwood gates.

The Walls shows what happens when all forms of art are integrated and you can enjoy Art Basel with a $5 beer. Those people who are pickier about how art is exhibited may not feel as special, but I'm more of a populist. I prefer art to be a tool of communication and therapy, wielded outside of the usual elitist spaces. It's fun.

And we are scoring on social media! Complain all you want about public art being reduced to a selfie backdrop, but not me. The way I look at it, if I have the **power to change the conversation by putting a subversive idea** in something that one might at first glance consider shallow, fine by me.

That's exactly what happened with my Obama poster. It was an **extraordinary viral explosion.** People may not know this, but it was never an official campaign poster; I wasn't hired or being paid by the Democratic Party. I just saw that people were feeling powerless and confused. Friends told me they weren't going to vote. It was my attempt to cut through the clutter with pure grassroots activism. The ubiquity of the poster proved that art has power. It affected people. It affected me. This year, I'm working on voter registration and exposing ways to elevate the truthfulness. With a little luck, I can help make America smart again.

Shepard Fairey creating one of Wynwood's only permanent murals, featuring its founder, Tony Goldman.

BRANDON OPALKA

"WE LIKE PAINTING **OUTDOORS** BECAUSE IT ENABLES US TO DIRECTLY INTERACT WITH **AN AUDIENCE** DURING THE PROCESS. **ULTIMATELY,** THE FINAL PRODUCT LEAVES A **POSITIVE,** LONG-LASTING IMPRÉSSION WITHIN THE COMMUNITY. IT'S OUR GIFT TO THEM. "

HOWNOSM, *Germany*

> **OPEN SPACE GIVES YOU THE FREEDOM TO BREATHE, THINK AND CREATE.**
>
> JESSICA GOLDMAN SREBNICK

"STREET ART IS AN ORGANIC FORM OF **EXPRESSION** THAT ALLOWS YOU TO USE **THE ENVIRONMENT** AS PART OF THE WORK. THE RESULT BRINGS COMMUNITIES TOGETHER, IT STARTS A CONVERSATION, **INFLUENCES AND INSPIRES.** WYNWOOD IS A MAGICAL PLACE LIKE A TREE THAT IS CONSTANTLY CULTIVATING **NEW LIFE.** IT IS A PLACE OF CREATIVE ENERGY AND GROWTH. "

SANTIAGO RUBINO, *Argentina*

FAFI
FAITH47
KASHINK
LADY AIKO
LADY PINK
LAKWENA
MAYA HAYUK
MISS VAN
OLEK
SHERYO

2013

WOMEN ON
THE WALLS

" THE THEME OF MY YEAR **CELEBRATED PREDOMINANTLY FEMALE ARTISTS,** WHICH HELPED DEBUNK **THE MYTH THAT WOMEN, IN ALL FIELDS, TRAIL BLAZE AFTER MEN.** THE REALITY OF **HUMAN NATURE** IS THAT WE'VE ALL WORKED TOGETHER AND INSPIRED ONE ANOTHER SINCE **THE DAWN OF THE SUN.** "

MAYA HAYUK, *USA*

MAYA HAYUK

Tony was a partner, a mentor and a good friend. My first office was in Tony's Park Central Hotel on Ocean Drive in South Beach. It was me alongside Tony, Mark Soyka and Leonard Horowitz. Now, if you go back to the beginning of Miami's renaissance, what was its single most important catalyst? It may sound weird and out of the box to say so, but it was Leonard's idea to paint all the Art Deco buildings in the area in pastel colors. Choosing this **specific palette made the buildings more photogenic**, and provoked a groundswell of interest and tourism.

In retrospect, our collective willingness to advocate for what Leonard proposed was a bigger deal than people think. In a way, if you look at what Tony chose as the catalyst for Wynwood, it was a variation on this simple yet clever concept. Instead of uniform pastels, he covered the exteriors of these buildings with commissioned graffiti. It was an **artistic, creative and adaptive** reuse of a proven marketing vehicle for an uninteresting collection of real estate properties. This brilliant reinterpretation captured an amazing audience.

CRAIG ROBINS

President and CEO, Dacra Real Estate Development

Tony also showed that great design doesn't have to be expensive. By turning unattractive warehouses into canvases, he tapped into the creative force of a new circle of artists, and it was a perfect fit. Tony gave Wynwood this amazing head start, and now Jessica is doing an outstanding job of implementing and expanding this vision. **Public art offers a platform** to all kinds of people who wish to express themselves with complete freedom and without judgment.

Wynwood's growth is an important moment in Miami's development because it highlights the options possible in this rapidly evolving city. The Design District is a different kind of creative neighborhood. It's more about graphic design and architecture. Brickell has been revitalized in a new, very urban way. Coral Gables is starting to undergo major changes. When you come to Miami, there are so many other unexpected places to go. It's not only about the beach.

A model posing in front of a wall being created by Kashink.

"I COULD SEE COLOR AND ENERGY AND EXCITEMENT EVERYWHERE. "

TONY GOLDMAN

ALEXIS DIAZ

CASE

CLEON PETERSON

CRYPTIK

DALEAST

FAITH47

HAAS & HAHN

KENNY SCHARF

POSE

REVOK

SHEPARD FAIREY

SWOON

TRISTAN EATON

2014

THE ART OF
COLLABORATION

I've been photographing street artists since I was a staff photographer for the New York Post in the seventies, when these kids created the art form. It was a renegade movement, like a secret society, and one reviled as well as dismissed by adults, and especially art critics.

But what they didn't see was that these kids have **incredible creativity.** All you had to do was go up to the Bronx where the Transit Authority houses the subway cars and see that their craft had quickly expanded from writing their names with style to include more imagery and social commentary.

I became obsessed with street art and wanted to photograph it, because this movement also had **its own sense of aesthetics.** Street art is adaptable to any medium. You can appropriate any space, and the process of observing artists like Olek, Vhils and HowNosm as they find that space, then gradually or maybe spontaneously turn it into art, is as creative as the finished work. **I find it too exhilarating not to capture.**

So I was thrilled when Tony offered to have me photograph the start of his new project and exhibit it as it was being formed. Following The Walls' evolution from an individual source of expression to what it's become has been fascinating. It's been amazing to watch this renegade movement turn into possibly the most popular art form in the world today.

MARTHA COOPER

Photographer, USA

Today's visitors are not traditional museumgoers. Often, they're ordinary people, from different cultures—families with their kids, coming to what may be their introduction to art in general. But even if they're here just to take selfies in front of a wall, they've devoted family time to this. The pictures wind up in their photo albums, on their social media accounts, and with any luck, will **serve as inspiration** for one of their kids to start drawing, choose an art class or at least become more aware of the unexpected that's always around us.

It's more impossible than ever to ignore. **Wynwood has inspired** a circuit of organized street art festivals around the world that stretches from New York's Coney Island to Spain's painted silos. Some are even bigger than Wynwood. But none of them has **the prestige and sense of community** that you find here. The Goldmans don't just offer space and a per diem to artists. Work here once and you are **forever part of the Goldman street art family.** I have made it my family, and no matter where else I travel to shoot, when I come back to Wynwood, I always feel as if it's "welcome home."

Wynwood's annual photographer, Martha Cooper, posing with an artistic likeness by artist David Choe, 2016.

"MOST IMPORTANTLY, THE WALLS AND ITS SURROUNDING STREETS OFFER A PLATFORM FOR AMBITIOUS YOUNG ARTISTS FROM ALL CORNERS OF THE WORLD."

HAAS & HAHN, *Netherlands*

"ACCESSIBILITY

WAS WHAT TONY PREACHED,

AND IT WORKED.
HIS BELIEF HELPED
SPREAD A
WORLDWIDE PHENOMENON. ''

KENNY SCHARF, *USA*

CRYPTIK AND DALEAST

FAITH47 AND ALEXIS DIAZ

SHEPARD FAIREY AND CLEON PETERSON

ALEXIS DIAZ
CASE
CRASH
CRYPTIK
EL SEED
ERNEST ZACHAREVIC
FAFI
HUEMAN
INTI
LOGAN HICKS
MAGNUS SODAMIN
PICHI & AVO
THE LONDON POLICE

2015
WALLS OF CHANGE

I was painting with the Primary Flight project in Miami in 2006 when I was lucky enough to catch Tony's attention. The urban street art scene was fairly new to me, and its acceptance was hardly universal. But Tony was the first one who treated me like an artist, not a street artist.

He showed me The Walls. He told me his plans, and I sat back and thought, "Oh shit, this is kind of going somewhere." This genre was just at the beginning, but this guy's ethos already had its future planned. Not only did it confirm my path, but Tony was right.

The foundation of Wynwood is the democratization of art. Unlike gallery owners, no one here tries to control you. They **let the artist make the art,** and the process is what drives the tourists. They come and see us working, straining and sweating, like self-employed blue-collar workers. They relate to that. They connect. We, in turn, get off on them, shoot the shit with them, with each other, and strive to create stuff the audience and our fellow artists have never seen before.

I was honored to paint under Tony. But I'm equally delighted to see the way Jessica has taken up the torch. There are now several mural festivals around the world, but Jessica is resolute that this will always be better than all of them, because she

LOGAN HICKS

Artist, USA

knows there's **more to it than just giving a painter a wall to paint on**. It's about offering artists a safe place to express what's in their heads and hearts. It's about merchandising, and it's about marketing. Those aren't dirty words. They're essential if you want to get your message out there and assure your relevance.

There are lots of other places we can get noticed now. I do sometimes worry that street art may be at the bursting point. Jessica's Global Arts program has us painting stuff on the walls of The Hard Rock Stadium. The attendance at Wynwood has quadrupled since I first came. Its reach is **explosive and instantaneous**, plus now it's global. Look at the emails, Facebook posts, and Instagram tags that keep popping up from Wynwood. I've signed on and seen Beyoncé, Jay-Z, Sylvester Stallone and Antonio Banderas standing in front of my work. Sometimes I feel like the backdrop. But at other times, I think, "Wow, these people want to be connected to my art." And that connection is why we're here.

Logan Hicks employing a stencil to create graphic detail on his 2015 mural.

IF WE KEEP UNIQUENESS AND SPECIALITY AND PLACE WITHIN OUR CITIES, WE ARE MAINTAINING THE CULTURE OF AMERICA.

TONY GOLDMAN

"THE STREET IS YOUR PORTFOLIO. IT'S THE ONLY ART MOVEMENT WHERE YOU ARE YOUR OWN CURATOR. YOUR ENERGY DRIVES YOU TO GO OUT, PUT YOUR ART OUT THERE AND SEE WHAT HAPPENS."

FAFI, *France*

"WHAT DISTINGUISHES **WYNWOOD** IS ITS PLANNING. IT'S THE PERFECT URBAN **STREET GALLERY** FORMAT, AND ARTISTS FROM ALL OVER THE WORLD REGARD IT AS A **GATEWAY** FOR THEIR WORK TO BE **APPRECIATED** IN ITS ORIGINAL CONTEXT."

INTI, *Chile*

"CREATING ART
IN THE STREET
FORGES A DIRECT
IMPACT
INTO PEOPLE'S LIVES.
WE BELIEVE ART
SHOULD ALWAYS BE
DRIVEN BY
EXPERIMENTATION
AND INNOVATION
TO KEEP PEOPLE
INTERESTED AND AWARE. "

PICHI & AVO, *Spain*

GRIT NEXT TO BEAUTY MAKES BEAUTY ALL THE MORE BEAUTIFUL.

TONY GOLDMAN

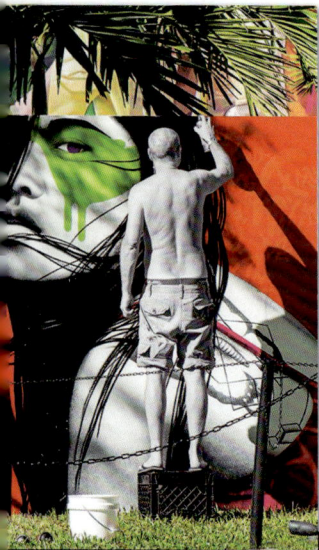

BEAU STANTON

DASIC FERNÁNDEZ

DAVID CHOE

FAITH47

FIN DAC

KEN HIRATSUKA

OKUDA

PIXEL PANCHO

RISK

TATIANA SUAREZ

2016

FEARLESS

I came to New York in 1982 on a grant from the Art Students League after having graduated from art school in Japan. I was already carving in stone by the time I was eighteen. I was immediately impressed by the graffiti all around the city. Within one month, I started carving conceptual art into the sidewalks of New York. The granite surfaces and the expanses of sidewalk felt like a challenge.

I've always been inspired by primitive art and architectural ruins. America is such a young country, it really doesn't have much awareness of primitive art. One day, I decided that the Earth was a big spherical rock floating in the universe and I would start carving a spiral in it and keep expanding until I covered the Earth in one continuous sculpture.

I started with a spiral in the sidewalk, on 21st Street, afraid of nothing, expanding continuously at intervals. People started noticing. I was onto something. In 2006, Tony bought a piece of slate I had etched. While I was traveling for a project in Mongolia, he called and left a message. He wanted me to carve the sidewalk in front of his new residential building at 25 Bond Street. I decided to carve it as one continuous line so that it was as if you were stepping into a rippling river.

Tony was so pleased, he invited me to Wynwood, then drove me around and showed me Kenny Scharf's and Futura's work at The Walls. Sure enough, when Tony expanded The Walls by buying the property next door, he bought the oversized boulders that were a fixture on the property and moved them by crane to a convenient place for me to begin working on them. I had to start early, because you can't carve stones quickly. It took two weeks for just one stone. Altogether, I invested six weeks on the project, finishing just when the other artists did.

I had never seen an outdoor museum like this, a shrine to street art and a celebration of its artists. It's amazing how he curated all of us, allowing us to do exactly what we wanted; he and his team treated all of us with such respect. It energized us to do something exceptional, because we felt as if we were at the Art Olympics. And there was Tony, walking around the space with Jessica as if he was at a great party.

I'm happy with how Jessica has sustained The Walls and taken them even further by encouraging and showcasing young artists in a space where their talent is immediately recognized and readily exposed to so many potential collectors. Tony had such an open love of art, and Jessica caught his rare spirit of appreciation and total support. I feel so lucky that there is this space that always wants me to reach a bit higher.

In 2012, I was honored when Janet Goldman asked me to design and execute Tony's gravestone—a testament to his creative spirit. Janet and I worked together to create a memorial that was lyrical, symbolic and bold. Made from more than twenty pieces of granite, Tony's tribute is in the shape of a wave, because waves, like love, never cease.

KEN HIRATSUKA

Artist, Japan

Ken Hiratsuka brushing of boulders in preparation for his work.

"**IT'S IMPORTANT** TO BE ABLE TO **COMMUNICATE** IN WAYS THAT PIERCE DIRECTLY **TO THE HEART AND SUBCONSCIOUS.** WE NEED TO BE ABLE TO **EXPRESS** AND UNDERSTAND EACH OTHER IN WAYS THAT **BREATHE WITHIN** THE REALM OF THE FANTASTICAL **AND ARCHETYPAL.**"

FAITH47, *South Africa*

"IT IS INCREDIBLE HOW YOU CAN **CHANGE** THE SKYLINE OF A CITY OR **INSPIRE** ANYONE PASSING BY, WHEN YOU MAKE **ART ESSENTIAL** TO THEIR ENVIRONMENT."

OKUDA, *Spain*

2SHY

AUDREY KAWASAKI

BORDALO II

EL SEED

FIN DAC

JOE IURATO

LADY PINK

LEON KEER

PRO176

RISK

SETH GLOBEPAINTER

TAVAR ZAWACKI

TRISTAN EATON

2017

HUMANKIND

When you first start creating art—in my case with woodcuts—you have to be doing it solely for yourself. That was my initial satisfaction. I never thought I would sell my work. But when I first came to Miami in 2009, I was just starting to sell in shows instead of just doing my work in the street. That was the first year of Wynwood Walls. The minute I saw that park, being part of it became my goal.

Logan Hicks is a good friend of mine and he introduced me to Jessica, and then she and her family started following my work. As much as I wanted it, I didn't see it coming when she finally asked me to be part of the 2017 show. It became a proving ground for me. Can I step it up? Is my work unique enough to be exhibited next to Shepard Fairey, Ron English, Logan and Futura?

When Jessica informed me that the show's theme was "humanKIND," I had an immediate connection. I decided that my kids—their playfulness, imagination and interaction— would be my inspiration. Using them was a first for me, but you have to challenge yourself when you're here, because the level of artistry around you is so high.

JOE IURATO

Artist, USA

But the atmosphere at The Walls is positive rather than competitive. Fafi showed me her stuff. Tristan Eaton, whose work I love, was nearby. David Choe was across from me. I fed off their high energy. Behind the scenes, at the hotel, all the artists would talk. Jessica set up dinners to get us together.

Jessica said, "Just tell me what you want." I said, "A thousand pounds of barn wood." And there it was. You dream it and then Jessica, Janet, Peter and the team will make it happen. All of this support combines to put you in this super special zone of creativity.

The show definitely solidified my career. First of all, creating something that is going to stand there for a few years raised my confidence. Plus, I was in the middle of Okuda and David Choe. Where else could I find such good company? New collectors found me. Galleries contacted me based on what they'd seen. My work became the backdrop for thousands of people on social media. As the art world expands, you are now part of the conversation. I painted a portrait of Janet. I found stability in my life. Jessica and her team took a gamble on me, and yet, I'm the one who really hit the jackpot.

Using paint and wood paneling, Joe Iurato creates three-dimensional and interactive art.

"WHAT STRUCK ME WHEN I PAINTED AT WYNWOOD WAS A SENSE OF CAMARADERIE, NOT JUST AMONG THE ARTISTS, BUT THE STAFF AND MANAGEMENT. EVERYONE JUST SEEMED GENUINELY HAPPY TO BE THERE, AND I FOUND THAT INFECTIOUS."

FIN DAC, *Ireland*

204   AUDREY KAWASAKI

> **"CATCHING THE ARTISTS PAINTING THE WALLS IS A SPECTACLE. TECHNICALLY, IT'S WATCHING PAINT DRY, BUT THE AUDIENCE AT WYNWOOD CAN'T STOP GUSHING ABOUT IT. FOR THE ARTISTS, THE EXPERIENCE IS FOOD FOR THE SOUL."**

TRISTAN EATON, *USA*

> "STREET ART GIVES YOU **THE FREEDOM** TO PAINT SCENES WITH MANY **SECRET MESSAGES,** YOU SEE SOMETHING **NEW AND MYSTERIOUS EVERY TIME.** WHEN ASKED TO PARTICIPATE **IN WYNWOOD,** I FELT REASSURED THAT ALL MY YEARS OF WORK FINALLY HAD **MEANING.** I JUDGE MY CAREER BY 'BEFORE' AND 'AFTER' WYNWOOD."

PRO176, *France*

> "WHAT HELPED EVEN MORE WAS THE COMPASSIONATE ENCOURAGEMENT FROM ONLOOKERS, FROM THE RESTAURANT EMPLOYEES, AND FROM THE PASSERSBY. THEIR INTERPRETATIONS AND ANALYSIS MOTIVATED ME AND TOUCHED ME."

SETH GLOBEPAINTER, *France*

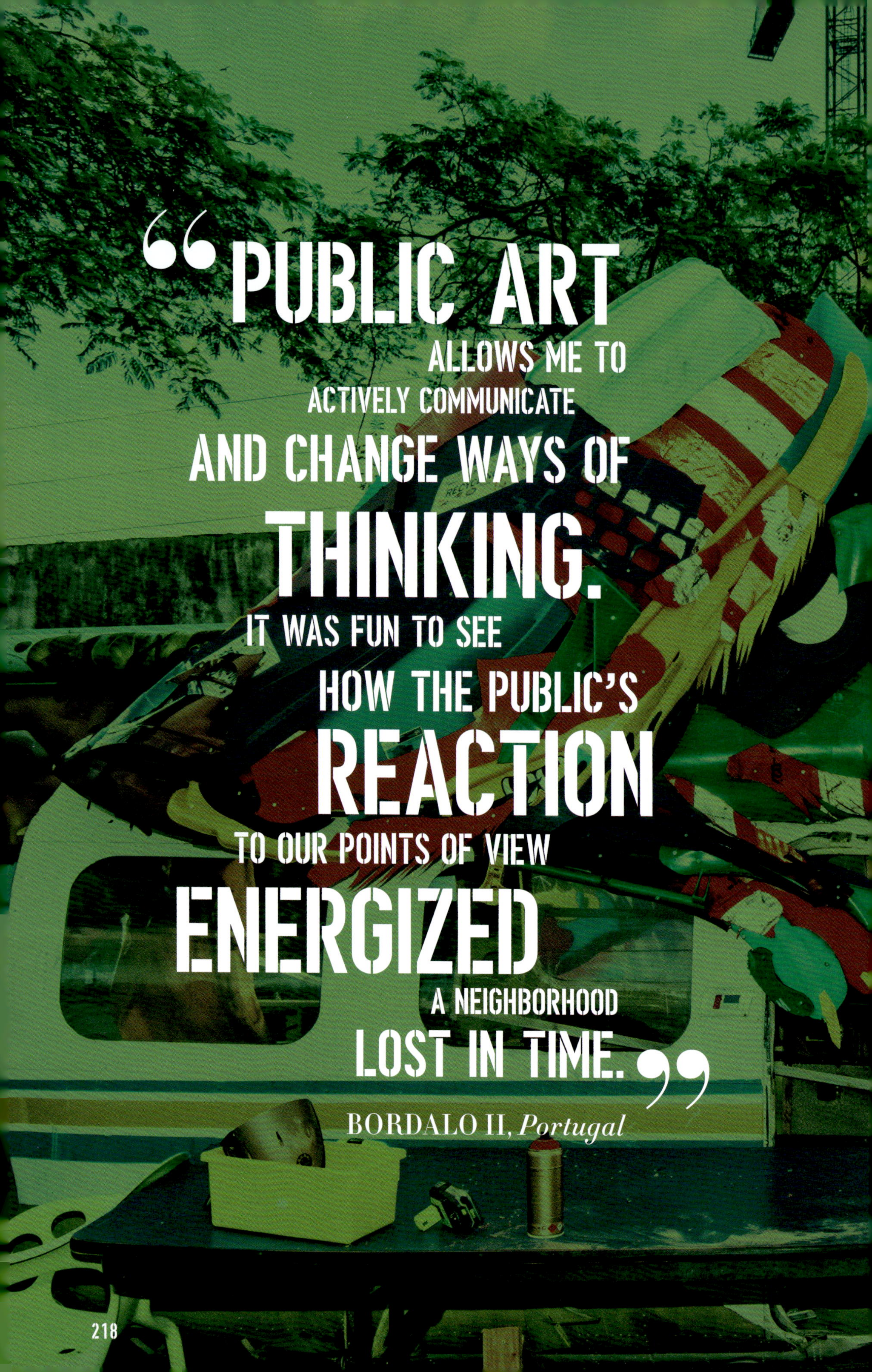

> ## "PUBLIC ART
> ### ALLOWS ME TO
> ### ACTIVELY COMMUNICATE
> ## AND CHANGE WAYS OF
> # THINKING.
> ### IT WAS FUN TO SEE
> ## HOW THE PUBLIC'S
> # REACTION
> ### TO OUR POINTS OF VIEW
> # ENERGIZED
> ### A NEIGHBORHOOD
> ## LOST IN TIME."

BORDALO II, *Portugal*

> **❝ IT'S AMAZING HOW ONE BLOCK CAN CHANGE THE LIFE OF A NEIGHBORHOOD. ❞**
>
> JANET GOLDMAN

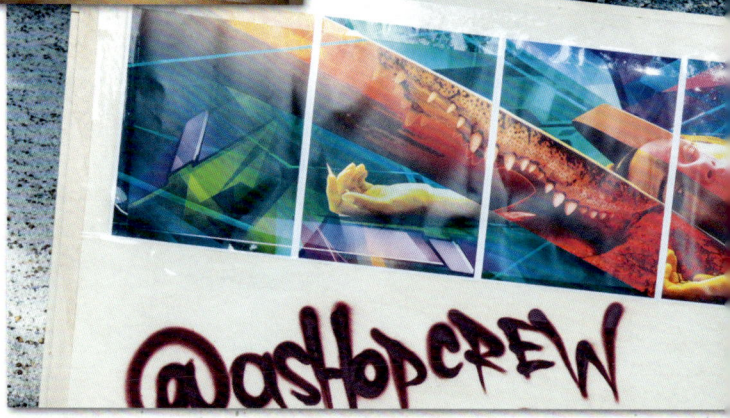

@ashopcrew

ASHOP CREW
DEIH
EDUARDO KOBRA
JONONE
MARTIN WHATSON
QUEEN ANDREA
RON ENGLISH
TOMOKAZU MATSUYAMA
VHILS

2018
BEYOND WORDS

I'm not really a muralist. I make really, really big paintings that are very detailed. Having shown at Art Basel for ten years, I'd watched the evolution of Wynwood into an artistic force some of us called **"The Street Art Olympics,"** so, when Jessica called me out of the blue in 2018, I said yes right away. But because of what I do, and how I do it, I told her that I would need more than just a few days to make something really special.

I showed up in Wynwood twelve days ahead of the opening, with four of my crew. The composition we proposed was pretty dynamic, built around a pair of horses and riders. We weren't going to work solely in spray paint. We used stencils. We used markers. We went so far as to work with paintbrushes so that we could detail flowers so intensely, you could see the veins in every petal of each cherry blossom.

TOMOKAZU MATSUYAMA

Artist, Japan

When we first starting working, people walking by kept asking, "Are you guys nuts?" I employed all I had learned in school studying both graphic design and fine art to keep adding layers of detail. Just when everyone thought we were done, we still had more to add. We were the first to show up every day and the last to leave.

OK, maybe we were nuts. But what's the point of participating if you're not going to do something people are going to talk about? Being part of Wynwood is another way of declaring there are no limits to what creative people can do. Yes, lots of fancy people come through and that is really impressive, but they stand alongside everyone else in this diverse, global melting pot. Then, after they are gone, what you see clearly is the creation of a neighborhood. A neighborhood created by art.

Tomokazu Matsuyama poses after completing his first Wynwood Walls mural.

"ALL THOSE FANS!
ALL THOSE
DIFFERENT LANGUAGES!
I WAS SURPRISED TO
MEET AND INTERACT WITH
SO MANY ONLOOKERS
FROM ALL OVER
THE WORLD.
IT WAS TRULY AN INTERACTIVE
INTERNATIONAL
EXPERIENCE."

QUEEN ANDREA, *USA*

"WORKING ON THE WALLS GAVE US THE **MOTIVATION** TO SURPASS OURSELVES AND GO OUT OF OUR **COMFORT ZONE.** IT GAVE US MORE **CONFIDENCE** IN OUR WORK AND HOW WE DEFINE OURSELVES AS ARTISTS. ART IS A VECTOR THAT **UNITES US ALL,** BYPASSING LANGUAGE AND BORDERS."

ASHOP CREW, *Canada*

“ IF YOU ARE LUCKY ENOUGH TO HAVE A PLATFORM, YOU HAVE A RESPONSIBILITY TO GENERATE GOOD. ”

JESSICA GOLDMAN SREBNICK

> "WHEN YOU WORK IN A VISUALLY SATURATED ENVIRONMENT, YOU HAVE TO CREATE A BIG IMPACT WHILE WORKING FAST AND WITH LESS ATTENTION TO DETAIL. IT'S MORE THRILLING THAN WORKING IN THE STUDIO. IT'S ONE OF THE BEST EXAMPLES OF THE POSITIVE IMPACT THAT ART CAN HAVE ON A COMMUNITY."

VHILS, *Portugal*

"IN A GALLERY, YOU REACH PEOPLE WHO SEEK ART. WHEN YOU PAINT IN THE STREET, YOU THROW YOURSELF IN FRONT OF PEOPLE'S EYES. THE WALLS IS A HUB FOR MEETING FELLOW ARTISTS, BUILDING RELATIONSHIPS AND SHARING IDEAS."

MARTIN WHATSON, *Norway*

MARTIN WHATSON

WYNWOOD WALLS ARTISTS

YEARS OF PARTICIPATION

ALEXIS DIAZ	2014, 2015	DEIH	2018
ARA PETERSON	2009	EDUARDO KOBRA	2018
ASHOP CREW	2018	EL SEED	2015, 2017
AUDREY KAWASAKI	2017	ERNEST ZACHAREVIC	2015
AVAF	2010, 2011	FAFI	2013, 2015
B.	2011	FAILE	2011
BARRY MCGEE	2009, 2010	FAITH47	2012, 2013, 2014, 2016
BÄST	2011	FIN DAC	2016, 2017
BEAU STANTON	2016	FUTURA 2000	2009
BEN JONES	2010	GAIA	2011
BORDALO II	2017	HAAS & HAHN	2014
BRANDON OPALKA	2011, 2012	HOWNOSM	2011, 2012
CASE	2014, 2015	HUEMAN	2015
CLARE ROJAS	2009	INTERESNI KAZKI	2011
CLEON PETERSON	2014	INTI	2015
COCO144	2010, 2011	INVADER	2010
CRASH	2015	IRAK	2011
CRYPTIK	2014, 2015	JEFF SOTO	2010
DALEAST	2012, 2014	JIM DRAIN	2009
DASIC FERNÁNDEZ	2016	JOE GRILLO	2011
DATE FARMERS	2011	JOE IURATO	2017
DAVID CHOE	2016	JONONE	2018
DAZE	2011, 2012	KASHINK	2013
DEARRAINDROP	2010	KEN HIRATSUKA	2016

KENNY SCHARF	2009, 2011, 2012, 2014
KRINK	2012
LADY AIKO	2009, 2013
LADY PINK	2013, 2017
LAKWENA	2013
LEON KEER	2017
LIQEN	2011
LOGAN HICKS	2010, 2011, 2015
MAGNUS SODAMIN	2015
MARTIN WHATSON	2018
MAYA HAYUK	2013
MISS VAN	2013
MOMO	2012
NEMEL	2012
NEUZZ	2011
NUNCA	2009, 2011
OKUDA	2016
OLEK	2013
OSGEMEOS	2009
PHASE 2	2010
PICHI & AVO	2015
PIXEL PANCHO	2016
POSE	2012, 2014
PRO176	2017
QUEEN ANDREA	2018
RETNA	2011
REVOK	2014
RISK	2016, 2017
ROA	2011
RON ENGLISH	2010, 2018
RYAN MCGINNESS	2010
SANER	2011
SANTIAGO RUBINO	2012
SEGO	2011
SETH GLOBEPAINTER	2017
SHEPARD FAIREY	2009, 2011, 2012, 2014
SHERYO	2013
STELIOS FAITAKIS	2009
SWOON	2009, 2014
TATIANA SUAREZ	2016
TOMOKAZU MATSUYAMA	2018
TAVAR ZAWACKI	2017
THE LONDON POLICE	2015
TRISTAN EATON	2014, 2017
VHILS	2011, 2018
2SHY	2017

ACKNOWLEDGMENTS

JESSICA GOLDMAN SREBNICK

This book is a story of daring, dauntlessness and dreaming. You need to believe in all three when you've resolved to think big, when you demand inclusivity, and when you refuse to be compromised by any limits or obstacles that might try to hinder this vision.

The Wynwood Walls began as our family's story. But today, every one of our participating artists has one they can tell as well, and the millions who visit The Walls offer still more. This book could not have happened without the willingness of so many of these amazing and committed people who have, and continue to, come together for a common goal of sharing, experimenting, creating and changing.

But there are several for whom our gratitude is eternal:

To Martha Cooper, our relentlessly curious and intrepid explorer, the one with the rare eye and a ready lens, who inherently knows just when to capture an indelible moment. No lift was too high, no rooftop too intimidating, no hour too early or too late. Martha is responsible for the visual history of our matchless cultural oasis. And if that's not enough, the artists trust and adore her.

To Jeffrey Deitch, for introducing my father, mother, brother and myself to this genre of art that became a lifelong passion for each of us, and for giving The Walls the jump-start ten years ago that sent us skyward.

To my husband, Scott, my love and admiration run through the deepest chambers of my heart.

To our sons, James, A.J. and Mack, being your mother continues to be my greatest joy. May you continue to build on the family legacy in your own way, with the foundations of creativity, passion, empathy and a solid work ethic.

To the Goldman Properties team, I derive such pride in being part of an organization of exceptional professionals who really are family to me. Your contributions have been, and continue to be, valued and deeply appreciated.

To my Goldman Global Arts team, this is just the beginning of our rocket ship ride to the stars.

To Monica Quiñonez, from conception to research, curation to execution, there is no way I could have done this book without you. It is our work of art.

To Peter Tunney, you look at every day as a beautiful adventure. I am forever grateful to be on this journey with you.

To Hal Rubenstein, for decades of friendship to our family and for your masterful ability to transform the simplest of words and ideas into a glorious symphony.

To the creative team of Assouline, led by Esther Kremer. I am delighted by and in awe of your collective ingenuity, inventiveness, patience and eagerness to collaborate in order to produce this startlingly beautiful book that gloriously represents our history, our currency and my father's legacy.

To the Wynwood Walls family of artists—we are a big, beautiful, global family. It has been the thrill of a lifetime and a life-altering education to know and love each and every one of you. Thanks to all of you for unhesitatingly sprinkling your magic dust on The Wynwood Walls.

To artists around the world, never give up on or discard your dreams. Your contributions to raising our collective human spirit are invaluable. Keep painting the world in all the colors of the rainbow.

To my brother, Joey, for your unflagging commitment to our family and our company. Your discovery of Wynwood was the spark that produced this global phenomenon.

To Mom—you are sunlight, shining on our family and everyone you encounter. You were Dad's greatest love and are my most cherished role model. A deeply accomplished businesswoman, mother, wife and friend, you are loved and admired by all, but most of all, by me.

To Dad—for a lifetime of magnificent lessons, limitless love and eternal optimism. Your spirit and energy are as vibrant as ever and your legacy lives on. The world thanks you for the gift of The Wynwood Walls.

JESSICA GOLDMAN SREBNICK, CEO of Goldman Properties, is a second generation leader of the company founded by her father, the late Tony Goldman. Since 2012, she has been the curator of The Wynwood Walls. In 2015, she co-founded Goldman Global Arts, a Miami- and New York-based creative collective. Jessica is an active member of the prestigious Young Presidents Organization, Vice Chair of the Town Square Neighborhood Development Corporation Board, and Miami Super Bowl 2020 Host Committee Co-Chair. Since 2010, she has participated in the YPO/Harvard Business School President's Program. In 2018, she was named one of Forbes' Icons of Impact. *@jessicagoldmansrebnick*

HAL RUBENSTEIN is the author of six books including the best-selling *100 Unforgettable Dresses*, one of the founding editors of *InStyle* magazine, where he served as its Fashion Director for fifteen years, a former men's style director of the *New York Times Magazine*, one of the founding editors of *Details* magazine, creator of the cult classic *Egg* magazine, and a former restaurant critic for both *Details* and *New York* magazine. In 2019, this CFDA Lifetime Achievement Award winner launched the multi-platform The Happy Grownup, which celebrates the excitement, possibilities and relevance of life after fifty. *happygrownup.com*

MARTHA COOPER is a Manhattan-based documentary photographer who has specialized in shooting urban vernacular art and architecture for over forty years. Her work has appeared widely in national and international publications. Martha's books include *Subway Art,* a collaboration with Henry Chalfant; *New York State of Mind*; *Tag Town*; *Tokyo Tattoo 1970* and *Remembering 9/11*. In 2009, Martha began photographing The Wynwood Walls while the first murals were being painted, and she has continued to document them every year since. *@marthacoopergram*

CREDITS

All images by © Martha Cooper with exception of the following: page 14-15: Brian Scantlebury Alamy Stock Photo; page 23: © Nika Kramer; page 26: Stephanie Jasper; page 64 top left: © Gary James; page 67: © Elizabeth Lippman; page 72-73: Elvis Suarez for GlassWorks MultiMedia; page 127: © Nika Kramer; page 194: Goldman Properties; page. 200-201, 202-203: Frank Mainade Jr; page 224: (center and bottom left) © Nika Kramer. Every possible effort has been made to identify legal claimants. Any errors and omissions brought to the publisher's attention will be corrected in future editions.

Cover: 2013 Mural by Maya Hayuk. Image by Martha Cooper.

© Goldman Properties
© 2019 Assouline Publishing
3 Park Ave, 27th Floor
New York, NY 10016, USA
Tel.: 212-989-6769 Fax: 212-647-0005
assouline.com

Art direction: Jihyun Kim
Design: Hannah Belken
Managing editor: Monica Quiñonez
Editorial direction: Esther Kremer
Editor: Lauren Ingram
Photo editor: Elizabeth Eames
Printed in Italy by Grafiche Milani
ISBN: 9781614288572